Dedication:

Chrysanthemum,
You were the most beautiful flower I had ever seen
I just had to have you for myself
I plucked you away from the garden
In which you had grown

But I am no florist
And as we both know
When you pull a flower from the ground

It dies

How arrogant of me to think
That here with me would be better
Than the home which made you into the masterpiece you are

You've since wilted away
And much like a dying flower
All I can do is preserve memory of you
In the pages of this book.

Like Father...

When I was 14
I told my parents I wanted to kill myself
My father
Said he didn't think I needed to see a professional
Everyone felt like that sometimes

And

Having something like that on file
Could ruin my life

So remember kids,
A ruined life
Is much worse than no life at all

So

If you can't overcome depression
All by yourself
At the ripe age of 14
Just
Go ahead and off yourself
Because there is no better option

Clarity

3 Months
It's been 3 months
90 days
2,160 hours

There hasn't been one second
Where you weren't on my mind
Sometimes
It's like you're a ghost
A memory I can barely hold onto
Others
It's like you're still right here
I guess thats what spending
Two years
Knee deep in addiction
Never fully present
Will do to you

Some memories are hazy
A dream you're trying to remember
But can't
Others are vivid
Like a nightmare you could never forget

But in sobriety I found clarity
And in clarity I've realized
The only common denominator
The only thing consistent
Throughout the dreams and the nightmares
Is you
And you're gone now
And I don't know I will ever be whole again

Rolecall

I always thought my life was a comedy
Turns out it's a tragedy

Likewise

I always thought I was playing the Hero
Turns out I'm the villain

Dimelo

Don't tell me
That I'm the love of your life
Don't tell me
That we'll always have each other
Don't tell me
That we'll get through this together
Don't tell me
That you love me, truly
Don't tell me
That if I was gone
Your life would "just stop"

Because I might do something stupid
Like believe you

And you might do what you always do
And leave

Crush

Our life together
Was like a cigarette
I had a craving
It hit the spot

With every puff it got hotter
Brighter
Such a satisfying burn
But then it was done
Burnt out
Nothing left but a small remnant
of what it once was
Something you throw away without a thought

Oh well
Better spark up another

But wait
My packs empty
And so is my wallet
I'm out of cash
Out of smokes
Out of chances.

Human

I am not a timebomb
I am a human being
A complex blend of carbon and
Some other stuff
My life isn't just
Counting down the days
Until an episode
Or an inevitable relapse
Or death
It's a journey
A story
My story

If I choose to learn from these things
If I choose to stay sober
If I choose to embrace my humanity
Then I am just that
A human

If i choose to ignore these things
And make no effort to grow
And learn
And change
To truly understand myself
And my shortcomings
Then I am a timebomb

I refuse to be a timebomb

Imperious

If you didn't want me broken
You don't get me fixed
If you couldn't stand to watch
While I struggled
Bent
And broke
You don't get to just
Come back
And tell me you're so proud
And that you've missed me
That maybe things
Can be different now

Because you
Couldn't stand by me
While I faced down my demons
While I laid in bed
Shaking from withdrawal

And when the shakes
Sweats
And vomiting subsided
You weren't there

When I started to find myself
I couldn't find you
When I finally got better
I was alone

So just stay gone
Because you don't deserve
The person I've become

Look to us

I thought the army would make me strong
No more episodes
No more falling apart
No more hating myself
I'm a soldier now
Why harm yourself when you can legally harm others?

Lean mean and green
U.S. Army fighting machine
Honorable
Loyal
Courageous
Selflessly serving my country

Except my platoon sergeant is cheating on his wife
With one of us privates
And our commander just got relieved
After his 3rd DWI

All these people want to do is chain smoke
And binge drink
This isn't what I wanted at all
This isn't what I needed
I wanted structure
And discipline
A purpose in life
To be part of something bigger than myself
To finally do something good

But all they tell me is
"You're such a boot
It's just a job
Get married so you can move out of the barracks
Have a kid, bank that extra BAH
DON'T EVER GET OUT YOU'LL REGRET IT"

Sometimes I miss my childhood
Despite all the trauma and abuse
I imagine this is the same thing

Impact

I never thought I'd lose you
For every fight there was a kiss
For every tear there was a smile
A constant push and pull of love and
Misunderstanding
Not hate
I could never hate you
I could never let you go
Not completely

I try every day as hard as I can
To let the thoughts of you drift away
Because I never thought that
After everything
I would be the one to get better
And you'd be the one to run

Sobriety has given me a new life
But I can't help but feel
Like its lackluster
Compared to the life I had with you
Your silly voices
Yelling at me to shut up
When I'm way too energetic in the early mornings
Spending entire sundays in bed
And not feeling like we wasted a second

I know I can never go back
But I can't help but wish
That you had come with me

Bombshell

I wish it had been anyone else
Anyone but you
Why did it have to be you
You were so different
The day I met you
I told myself
"You're gonna marry that girl"

I've been with plenty of people
More than I'd ever care to admit
So why did it have to be you
Why are you the one
Who I built a life with
And then destroyed it
Why did you have to be the one
To make me realize I had a problem
Only for it to already be too late
You've already moved on
No more chances

I wish it would have been anyone else
But I know that if it had been
It wouldn't have been enough
Losing you was the only thing that shook me enough
To finally fix myself
But living life without you
Is the only thing
That's ever made me want to use again

I guess life's just funny like that

York Beach

I hope you're happy
Wherever you are
Whoever you're with
I hope you're bursting with joy

I hope every morning you wake up
With no doubt in your mind
About if he loves you
If he's clean
Where he was last night

I hope every night you go to sleep
Completely assured
That your life is what you know it to be
And that you're exactly where you need to be

I hope when thoughts of what I did drift into your mind
They're snuffed out
By your confidence in him
And when the damage I did starts to show
Its quickly repaired
By the love and trust
You've built with him

I hope you become the person
I've always known you can be
And no matter what
Above all else
I hope you're happy

Me @ me

It's not about
Liking a picture
Or making a comment to your friends

Why is expressing your lust for someone else
More important to you
Than your partner's trust and security

Let's be clear
Absolutely no one
Is under the delusion
That you find only one person
Out of the billions on the planet
Attractive

But why
Is being able to acknowledge
How hot someone else is
So fucking important to you
That you'll hurt the person you love
And when they speak up
You'll tell them
"You're too insecure
Don't be so controlling
You really need to grow up"

Is destroying your lovers self esteem
Really worth the "freedom"
To lust after someone who
Most likely
Doesn't even know you exist?

Who knows?

What is love?
Is it the same for everyone?
Is it real?
Do we all really experience the exact same feeling?

Or is it just and idea?
Something we all chase
And claim to have known
Something we just
Invented one day
To make life more bearable
And it caught on
And everyone started saying
"True love trumps all
Love is all you need
What's life without love?"
And no one wanted to admit
They had no idea what everyone else was talking about
So they just smiled
And nodded their heads
Of course they knew what love was

Did evolution make a mistake
When we became aware of how insignificant our lives are?
And the only way
For the entire species not to just lay down and give up
At the hands of that knowledge
Was to invent some overwhelmingly amazing feeling
That for some reason
No matter how awful life got
Would make it all worth it in the end

Or is it real?
Is it something we'll never be able to understand or explain?
But when you know you know
When you see someone you love
Your body just feels different
When you two embrace
It's like the whole world is spinning just for you
And no matter how bad things get

You have each other
And this magic feeling
Gives you strength
And hope
When you deserve neither

I don't know what love is
But as far I can tell
Whether it's just chemicals in our brains
Or some divine spiritual connection we will never truly understand
It's enough

Reality Check

Sometimes
It takes ruining the best thing you've ever had

To realize
You're the worst you've ever been

I'm sorry

Imagine going back
And meeting yourself at 14
Imagine having to break it to that poor kid
That it's not even close to over
That adolescence is just the beginning
That there is so much more pain on the horizon

It'll be almost a decade
And he'll have become
A veteran
An addict
A cheater
A survivor
A failed artist
And an accomplished liar

And after ruining everything
After hurting everyone
He will finally get it
He was the problem

Here's lookin' at you, kid

Pupil

You were born with your own set of eyes
Stop trying to look at yourself
Through everyone else's

Well, do you?

Do you think he knows?
When he lays down next to you
Do you think he knows?
That he's laying next to the love of my life
Do you think he knows?
About the words you wrote me just before you left

Do you think he knows?

That no matter how far you go
Part of you is always here with me
In the letters I kept
And the photos I can no longer stand to look at
But I can't just throw away
Those moments frozen in time
Of you smiling, and happy
When we still had a chance
Locked in a drawer since the day you left

Do you think he knows?

Spyglass

On the days I find myself
Wandering through my past
I usually am faced with only one question

What was I thinking?

And on those days especially
I have to remind myself
That the clarity to look back
And see my own flaws and mistakes
Is what I have worked so hard for

The victim or the perpetrator

I don't remember which came first
Wanting to kill myself
Or doing anything and everything I could get my hands on

I don't remember which came first
Making jokes constantly about suicide
Or the comforting feeling that I was a bad enough person
No one would really miss me anyways

I don't remember which came first
Negative self image as a worthless disgusting waste of a person
Or
Negative self image as a horrible evil monster of a human

I don't remember which came first
Being sad or being bad

I tell myself all the terrible things I've done
Were only me trying to feel better
But the truth is

I don't remember which came first

Night Terror

Imagine
Trying to get over someone
Except every night you work it out
And fall back in love

And you're literally pinching yourself
And slapping yourself in the face
Because
You don't remember driving to her house
Or knocking on her door
Or walking up to her room

But you can't seem to wake up
So you let yourself believe it
Everything's fixed

And that's when your alarm goes off
It's 6am on a tuesday morning
You're a recovering addict
And she's had you blocked for months

Fault Line

It's not my fault
That I'm messed up
It's not my fault
That I dissociate
That the only way I found
To cope with everything that happened to me as a child
Was to invent a completely different person
Someone who could break my boundaries, and bend my morals

No
I didn't ask for this
It's not my fault

However

Fixing it is my responsibility
The neighbor
Who Thought I was just the sexiest 4 year old he had ever seen
Isn't going to come back and pay for my therapy
The kids who bullied me in middle school
Because my voice didn't start to chance until I was 14
Are not going to say sorry now

No

None of that is my fault
But using people
That was my fault
Drinking my problems away from 16 to 22
That was my fault
Lying to everyone abou where all my money went
And why my exes had left me
That was my fault

I didn't ask to be abused
But neither did anyone else
And the only way to break the cycle
Is to accept that although I'm not the one who broke me
I'm the only one who can fix me

Veil

The thing about recovery
Is once you start it doesn't stop
You had your first breakthrough
When you went to that first meeting
Walked into that therapists office
Left that abusive home

But

You didn't have your real breakthrough
Until you went back

Maybe you took a sip
Maybe you started browsing the back pages
Maybe you texted your old dealer

However close you got
You realized
You're different now
You're no longer someone
Living in reaction to a troubled past
You're no longer able to convince yourself
That this will help
And even if you do pull the trigger
You've now seen the difference
Between making a fully self aware bad decision
And a quick knee jerk attempt to self medicate

And after that you could never really go back
You haven't just pulled back the veil

You've burned it

Girls and Boys

I think I love you
In the most innocent way possible
Your smile makes my day
But the thought of my lips against yours feels wrong
As if the sky were to come down and touch the earth

I think I love you
The way a toddler loves their teddy bear
Sitting next to you on the couch or in the car
Is the safest I have ever felt
But the idea of you laying on top of me feels foreign
Like wearing your shoes on the wrong feet

I know you're a beautiful woman
And I am not so bad myself
But I think I love you
In the strongest
Most platonic way possible
So please don't ever leave
Or I'll be like the earth without the sky
Or a child without their bear
Or perhaps
Just a man
without his best friend

Executioner

Most mornings it's difficult Just to wake up
Alone in our bed
To start my day
Every day
With the knowledge that I hurt you so bad
The only way you saw to heal
Was to separate yourself from me so completely

The way a guillotine would separate a head from its body
I can see you rolling away
Just a fraction of what you used to be
All I can do is stand and watch
With your blood on my hands

What have I done?

East High and Dry

I don't hate you for moving on
I was nothing worth your while
I don't hate you for loving him
Everyone says he's great
I don't hate you
Period

But I don't like you
Because you lied to me
And I don't like you
Because you lied about me
And I don't like you most of all
Because you said you would always be there
Over and over you told me
"We're a packaged deal"

And now I'm damaged goods
And you're a work of art
I'm a milkshake dropped on the sidewalk
And you're a graffiti masterpiece

I'm nothing and you're everything
And why would everything ever bother
To apologize to nothing

Halfblood Zero

I think I always loved Greek Heroes
Because no bad deed couldn't be undone
Hercules murdered his entire family
And spent the next decade kicking ass and taking names
Then became a god

I always wanted life to be like that
Where my mistakes lead to adventure and fame
Not heartache and pain

All I'd have to do is go fight some beast
Sacrifice some animal to the gods
And bam!
Everyone loves me again

Unfortunately my life seems to be more like that of a medieval knight
Disgraced, stripped of my honor, cast out by my lord
All I can do is wander the wilderness
Trying to live as pious as possible
In hopes that one day I'll be absolved
After my death

Self Reflection

Sometimes
I spend hours staring at myself in the mirror
Trying to recognize the person staring back

Sometimes
I catch a glimpse of myself passing by a storefront window
And I've never felt more secure

Take 2, and Call me a liar

They say secrets keep you sick
And the truth is only medicine

But no one's life shatters when you take antibiotics
My mom never said
"What happened to my baby boy?!"
Because I got a flu shot
I didn't just catch a cold
Part of me always knew what I was doing

Is coming clean really fair?
Is hurting everyone who cares about me
Just so I can dump my guilt
Really fair?

Or am I just afraid
Terrified of ruining my reputation
So I justify keeping my secrets
Telling myself that I'm protecting everyone
Like trying to polish a bronze medal
To a point where it might resemble gold
Maintaining the facade
Constantly
Every day

They say secrets keep you sick
They're right

Alone with me

I think being alone terrified me
Because you were my only reason to stop
And I think that's why I could never stop

I'd be good for a while
But then the parts of me
That I was using you to hide from
They'd find me

So
I'd lie to you
And everyone else

But it wasn't until I was truly alone
And had no one left to lie to but myself
That I realized
I don't want to live like this

I thought your love would fill the empty parts of me
But I wasn't just empty
I was broken
Like a cup with a hole in the bottom
Nothing could ever fill it
Until I patched the hole

My Last

You are my last
I wanted it to stay that way
I wanted you to be my last kiss
The last hand I'd ever hold
The last person I'd ever wake up next to

To this day you are still my last
But I am not yours
Not for a long time
And sitting here holding on is killing me

You're a cinder block tied to my ankle
And I'm drowning
But I can't find the resolve
To sever my own foot and live

Letting you go means leaving a piece of me behind
Letting you go means you'll never be my last
Letting you go means surviving
Letting you go means learning to live
Without the piece of me that I'll leave with you

Am I really strong enough for that?

Fairy Tales and Farewells

Being with you was like
Living in a fairy tale
Our story was incredible
We had fought so hard to be together

I remember us laying there
On the futon in my first apartment
Just holding each other
On the brink of tears
We had finally done it
Your parents had given us their blessing
No more hiding
No more sneaking around
No more lying to our families
We could finally just be together

Yes,
Our story was one for the ages
But it was just that
A story
And I know that getting over you
Means letting go of that story
Our story
Letting go of the belief
I've clung so tightly too over these past years
That you and I were meant to be
That everything we went through
In the last 60 months
Was all worth it
Because no matter what
We would always have each other

But now,
All I have left of you is this story
This tale playing out in my head
A narrative I built a long time ago
To hide from the truth
That we
were so obviously
Never meant to be

That's all.